# BECOMING
# A
# GOOD
# ANCESTOR

EMOTIONAL WISDOM FROM
A LIFE LIVED THROUGH WAR TO FORGIVENESS

ALEXANDRA ASSEILY

Published by ZULU BOOKS

Cover design by Vibol Moeung
Illustrations by Juan Carlos Osorno

ISBN: 978-1-3999-8642-7

Printed and bound in London by P2D Books

*To my wonderful family and friends from far and wide – and those throughout my life who've helped me to navigate both the fun and the challenging bits. You know who you are.*

# ABOUT THE AUTHOR

Born Alexandra Durlacher in Malta in 1937, Alexandra Asseily is a psychotherapist and spiritual thinker whose experience of conflict has inspired a lifelong commitment to peace and forgiveness.

Alexandra's father (Admiral Sir Laurence Durlacher) was of British and Jewish descent, while her mother (Rimma Sass-Tisovsky) came from a Russian-Ukrainian Orthodox family who emigrated from Kharkiv, Ukraine to Mougins, France in 1920 during the Russian Civil War. She grew up in Malta, Singapore, and the UK, where she lived through the Blitz in the Second World War.

In 1969, Alexandra married George Asseily, a Lebanese Greek-Orthodox businessman, and moved to Beirut. As a witness to the pain of Lebanon's civil war (1975–1990), she began to explore her own responsibility for war and peace, which led her to train as a psychotherapist. Her professional training covered a broad set of disciplines including Jungian Psychotherapy, Neuro-Linguistic Programming, Educational Kinesiology, and Psychology of Vision.

In 1998, Alexandra initiated the Garden of Forgiveness (Hadiquat as Samah) in downtown Beirut, a project to create a garden in the heart of the city to facilitate forgiveness and reconciliation for the various communities in Lebanon and beyond. The project has been designed and agreed but is awaiting implementation.

In 2011, she began leading a series of workshops in Lebanon, titled Healing the Wounds of History: Addressing the Roots of Violence, to highlight transgenerational trauma and the importance of forgiveness. In the Healing the Wounds of History programme, attendees explore and uncover the depth of their own and others' traumatic memories and pain, whether experienced or unconsciously inherited. They are then taken through specific exercises to uncover a new, innate understanding of themselves and 'the other'. The training has transformed the lives of hundreds of people of different ages, religions, and ethnicities from Lebanon, Syria, Rwanda, the United States, and beyond.

In line with her vision for peace and reconciliation, Alexandra has co-founded a number of initiatives, including: the Centre for Lebanese Studies, Oxford; the British Lebanese Association; and the Ara Pacis Initiative for Peace, Rome. She is also a long-time board member of the Guerrand-Hermès Foundation for Peace; a former member of the Leadership Council at Harvard Divinity School; a former member of the Advisory Board of the Centre for the Study of World Religions at Harvard University; and a life-long member of Subud, a spiritual movement that emphasises the experience of direct personal connection with the divine.

Alexandra has five children and fourteen grandchildren. She lives between the UK and Lebanon, where in 2000 she co-founded the Silk Museum with her husband George Asseily on the site of a restored nineteenth-century silk factory near their home in Bsous.

# FOREWORD

Our ancestors had a much stronger sense of the circle of life, the passing of the seasons and years. It was hardwired into the social calendar, the rituals, and the rites of passage. It was the glue that held together communities. Stories were preserved, embellished, cherished, and shared oral traditions passed on by the fire. My father once said to me that one of the hardest things about losing your parents is the realisation that you are now the story bearer. Perhaps this is why, in the second half of our lives, so many of us become obsessed with family history. We find ourselves wanting to walk where our ancestors walked, to handle objects that they handled.

With technology, it is becoming easier to pick up these trails, the fragments of memory, the indestructible links. But it is harder to preserve what these characters stood for – their values – beyond the apocryphal tales of distant relatives. We form a sense in our family narratives about the recent ancestors who have done most to shape us. But despite all the search-engine-propelled research, we tend to know less about our great-grandparents than they did about theirs. Our sense of community and calendar has been bent into a different shape by several centuries of urbanisation and several decades of globalisation. Netflix and decent central heating have replaced the campfire.

Yet part of honouring and remembering our ancestors is to protect and pass on the best of what they left us, including the best of their values. Somewhere along the way, did we forget what it meant to be a good ancestor?

While in Lebanon and since, I became fascinated by the work of Alexandra Asseily. At its core, her outlook is based on a simple idea: that our ancestors' role in conflicts affects us psychologically, influences our relationships with family and friends, and contributes to our propensity – or not – to participate in the next wave of strife and pass it on again to the next generation.

If Alexandra is right, we bear a huge responsibility for whether, through our beliefs and behaviour, we transmit these traumas and grievances to our children, an inheritance that has far more potential to shape their lives than the contents of a will. Similarly, we can see ourselves as receivers of inherited patterns and traumas, echoed from conflicts rooted before our time. Alexandra believes that it is possible, as individuals and communities, to address these deep-set traumas and intolerances, and to make it easier for broken groups to reconcile.

For Alexandra, this means we must ask ourselves some difficult questions:

> *How do we become good ancestors and refrain from passing on trauma or negative beliefs to future generations? How do we stop being the prisoners and the puppets of the stinging memories of strife that we can still feel today as though we ourselves were present at that first event? How do we clean up what I call our 'ancestral arteries' so that our children are free to act in the now, free from the blocks which echo from the past, and clog up our todays and our tomorrows, and be able to receive our collective talents and gifts instead?*[1]

This book goes some way towards answering these questions, as well as how we can live a peaceful and fulfilling life. The healing process can also involve probing our family memories and stories, what Alexandra once told me is a 'great architectural dig':

> As with archaeology, we find things buried, which require our knowing, acknowledging, and understanding, as well as a 'carbon dating' in order to reveal how, and why, they were hidden and buried. All families have ghost stories: the difficult or troubled individual, the moment when someone was rejected or driven away. As we bring these old elements to the light, they can be appraised with love and trust, rather than by judgement or fear. It becomes possible to release old and ancient grievances.[2]

By doing this, we can find ways to ensure that our personal, family, or community's history informs but does not control us. We can discover the scars in our family's past that have never properly healed and, consequently, we can give our descendants a better chance of moving beyond them.

This is where the science meets the politics of building a better society. In peace-making or rebuilding post-conflict communities, we are often dealing with the legacy of previous conflicts. These conflicts might have taken place long before those involved in the peace process were born. In diplomacy, there is space for understanding the collective psychology of a nation – in other words, for trying to be the nation's therapist. And indeed the words you try to use, the tone of connection, the people you bring together, sometimes do feel like an act of collective therapy.

---

[1]Asseily, Alexandra. 2007. *Breaking the Cycles of Violence in Lebanon – and Beyond*. Brighton: Guerrand-Hermès Foundation for Peace Publishing, page 6.
[2]Asseily, Alexandra. 2019. Private conversation with Tom Fletcher.

In Alexandra's work – distilled into this short but powerful book – lies the key not just to living well and becoming good ancestors, but to the future of diplomacy, peace-making, and ultimately, human survival. Her ideas are truly transformational.

**Tom Fletcher, 2024**
Principal, Hertford College, Oxford
Former UK ambassador to Lebanon
Former foreign policy adviser to prime ministers Tony Blair, Gordon Brown, and David Cameron

# CONTENTS

# INTRODUCTION

Dear reader,

This book is a collection of my ideas, reflections, and wonderings on life over the years. These thoughts might appear random at first, much like life, but they gradually open a path to healing.

We are all born innocent. We are then shaped by our ancestry, our collective memory, our trauma, and our educators. But we still have a choice. We can be fearful in taking the next step, or courageous. We can accept our inheritance passively and unconsciously, or we can have the courage to move beyond it.

I've been very lucky in my life to have people around me who believed I could not just take the next step, but make great leaps. It often only takes the encouragement and patience of a few people to open us up to the possibilities of life and to direct our courage so that we can grow.

We each have the capacity to become masters of our own universe. The first step is to become inquisitive – or, as Gabor Maté says brilliantly, to develop *compassionate inquiry* about our life, our thoughts, our feelings, and those around us. We can then begin to accept our unique qualities and give them a chance to grow and flourish.

Once we begin to become more compassionate towards ourselves and others (no matter how terrifying or 'alien' they appear), we expand our capacity to love. We give our children – and indeed all those we've touched – the chance to become more tolerant, creative, and loving. We also, more importantly, help to heal the world.

My hope is that this little book can help you take your own journey through life with joy and fulfilment and, in time, become a good ancestor.

With love always,

Alexandra

# Strive for Greatness, Not for Perfection

I f you're going to do something, do it to the best of your ability. I remember, clear as a bell, my woodwork teacher showing me the correct techniques for preparing or finishing a piece of work, assuring me that I could ask any questions in order to learn, take care, and do it right.

This instilled a pride in my woodwork, which eventually flowed over into the rest of my life. By its very nature, putting my heart and soul into my work meant my unique, imperfect qualities were embedded in the results. I learnt to embrace this rather than to strive for an abstract sense of perfection – in all aspects of my life.

So do not strive for perfection, because it is unattainable. Rather, do things with pride, integrity, and to the best of *your* abilities. And, above all, have patience in your capacity to reach the right place over the perfect place.

# Love and Let Bloom

L et plants show you how to be yourself in the best way.

I was never taken by the perfectly ordered French style of gardening. I don't want to strangle my plants into being something they're not or cap their growth before they've shone.

It's the same with people. You don't tell someone how to bloom. You give them everything they need and watch them bloom in their own way.

In my garden you'll find glorious roses proudly blooming over an old tree stump on a floor of bluebells. One looks composed, the other is wild and free. Both are as Mother Nature intended, and both are perfectly happy blooming in their own special way.

It's the same with children, employees, partners, and teams. Give them what they need to feel safe, secure, and happy, and let them bloom in their own way.

Give them space and, if they need it, guidance and nurturing.

# Friendship

Find a companion.

It could be a family member, friend, or colleague. At any stage of your life.

Sometimes when you're feeling low that's all you need.
Find someone and let them be kind to you.

There's beauty in letting that happen.

A beautiful person in my life who was an amazing companion was Fadel, a tall and charming Lebanese man from South Beirut. He was hired as a driver for our family but, in time, he became far more of a friend and companion to me. We talked a lot. He was a kind, patient, and lovely man. Everyone loved and trusted him, and his presence made me feel safe, understood, and not alone.

Friendships can grow from shared experience or shared adventure, but they don't need to be your entire world.

If you stick to the same group of people you knew as a child, or at school, or in any specific place or time, you will miss out on the great variety of life and the possibilities of what it can provide. Great friendships are about feeling understood and understanding the other.

They are also about playfulness and adventure – in thought, word, or deed.

Great friendships encourage the best in us to flourish, without letting us get away with our bullshit for too long. Grow your friends in various soils: some to laugh with, others to debate politics and history with, some to play sports with, and others with whom to expand your spirituality.

Don't be frightened of making friends in strange places. Develop your friendships in all directions – and you'll grow with them. Allow them to ebb and flow with the seasons of life and tend to them not through duty or obligation, but through mutual reward and fun.

Be brave and adventurous with your friendships. Love will expand naturally to reach them all.

# Religion

I don't deny any religion at all.

When I pray, I don't pray to any particular god; I trust that the right one will be listening and will advise or connect with me somehow – through a message, an instinct, a feeling, or a vision.

Tolerance for others means that 'God' can be different for all of us.

I find beauty in them all.

# Taking a Leap

If you're ever fearful of being judged, work hard, and do whatever it is to the best of your ability. You can be pleased with what you've achieved, humble receiving feedback, and proud to move forward.

You need to get out of your comfort zone to make your mark.

I was terrified when my first piece of academic work was released when I was in my forties; I'm not an academic at all! However, I worked so hard and believed so strongly in what I did that I knew I could debate the subject with anyone.

Even though not everyone agreed with me, that leap of faith allowed me to meet extraordinary people who opened doors that led to so much goodness in my life and in the world. I can't even think about what would have happened if I hadn't leapt, if I'd stayed in my comfort zone... I wouldn't have become *me*.

When we only live for such a short time, hesitating to take that leap is tragic.

Do *your work* and be prepared. Trust that your work will find the right audiences and attract the right feedback so it can evolve and improve.

But first, take the leap.

# Tiny Acts Towards Success

Nelson Mandela said, 'It always seems impossible until it is done.'

I agree with him wholeheartedly.

If you're ever faced with a gargantuan task, remember that success is made up of many tiny acts all coming together. It might take years of hard work, training, and meeting people to make something big happen. Much of this is hidden from the view of others.

However easy it might seem to those admiring the finished item, it never is. Success rarely comes out of the blue.

Make a plan, see where it guides you, and maintain the resolve, patience, and determination to see it through.

# Good Chaos, Not Certainty

It's absurd for you to know everything that can happen.

You will never have that certainty. No one does.

Do your best to feel your way through. Have a vision, work towards it, but – more importantly – *engineer good chaos*. Become comfortable with uncertainty. Not only is it natural but it can produce amazing, unimagined outcomes.

In a team, work with good people who come together – despite challenges and doubts – to find solutions that bring sense to whatever the next step may be.

As a leader, give people what they need to be themselves; make space for randomness and creativity to flourish. Good things will happen if you share the same good intentions and trust in others' respective contributions.

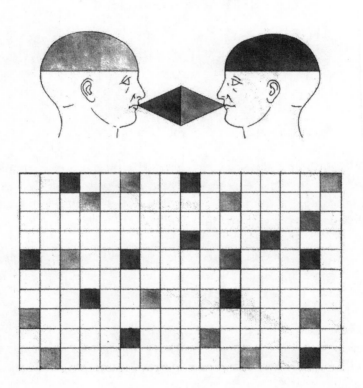

# The Power of Language

Everyone is fighting their own inner battles, so be kind to others – including yourself. You never know the extent of the impact you'll have.

Many years ago, a Colombian friend of mine was concerned about her daughter, who was dyslexic and struggling with judgement from others. My friend asked me to help. Her daughter and I spent time together working on her language and how she spoke to herself (in other words, her inner voice).

When we reminisced about this twenty years later, she still remembered every word I'd taught her. I was amazed that the short time we'd spent together had had such a profound effect on her life. Knowing that my words could reach people to that extent was both sobering and revealing.

Words can transform lives and move nations. Choose them carefully.

Language can be divisive, victimising, and bullying. Or it can be cohesive, integrated, and constructive. Either way, it is a potent force for change.

Authoritarian language is humiliating, pressurising, and guilt-inducing. In internal or external dialogue, it creates stress, rebellion, resentfulness, shame, a sense of failure, and self-sabotage or blame. It creates subdued or 'good children', who often resent the pressure to be 'good' or become enraged and vengeful. It is fear- and ego-based.

Positive language is trusting and encouraging. It frees us from authoritarian pressure, energises us to act freely without conflict or stress, and enhances our attitude towards ourselves and others. It strengthens our body–mind system, it helps us understand the roots of old or ancestral grievances, and it opens us up to forgiveness – both for ourselves and others.

It all starts with how you speak to yourself.

The language we use to speak to ourselves is as important as the language we use to speak to others. If we judge, bully, or attack ourselves with our internal dialogue, we are more likely to judge, bully, or attack those around us. We are also more likely to attract attack. Positive language frees us from the cycle of blame, violence, and victimisation.

To start using the language of positive authority, it helps to first notice the dynamics and dangers of authoritarian language and how it affects your well-being and society.

You can then begin to change your own internal dialogue and adopt and use the language of positive authority. For example, instead of 'should', use 'can': instead of 'you should have done better at this', try 'I believe you can do your best'.

Finally, share and promote positive language.

As we learn to change our language – and the feelings that go with it – from authoritarian, stress-based language to positive authority language that uses the whole brain (i.e. right and left hemispheres together), we help to free ourselves, our families, our friends, and our co-workers from cycles of violence.

This costs no money, takes no time, and requires only personal responsibility and gentle vigilance.

All this brings to mind a classic but apt story.

> *An old chief was sitting around the fire with his grandchildren, teaching them about the ways of life.*
>
> *At one point, the old chief told them gravely, 'There is a battle going on in my heart between two lions. One is fear, distrust, aggression, isolation, self-interest, envy, and war; the other is courage, loyalty, friendship, truth, generosity, solidarity, and peace.' Then he added, 'It is a fierce battle and it is taking place within each one of us.'*
>
> *The children stood silent, then one asked, 'And which lion will win?'*
>
> *The chief answered, 'The one you feed.'*

# In the Being, the Doing Gets Done

*"Love is not something you do;*
*it is just the way you are"*
— SADHGURU.

While I was looking for antiques in Cairo, someone recommended I find a man called Abbu. A little boy offered to take me. After two hours winding through the streets of Cairo, we came to a cavernous shop with no signs. Inside, sitting in the darkness, were two men. I was immediately struck by the presence of one man in particular. He was very young and dressed in white, like a sheikh.

I became instantly aware that this man was complete.

He was whole, with no ego. He was simply being himself, a human being.

As he met my gaze, I heard myself say, 'The sheikh has holy eyes.'

That moment of consciousness triggered something inside. I returned later, certain that the sheikh had been sent to give me a message. As I crossed the threshold back into the shop, I realised that I had already received it: *in the being, the doing gets done.*

I thanked him and cried, releasing centuries of guilt of doing – or not doing – instead of just being.

There's a hint in the name of our species: human being.

I was brought up with the guilt, for me rooted in Christianity, of 'having to do something good' in order to be a worthwhile human being. Having to be good or having to save someone – the 'having to' puts so much pressure on our external behaviour, it's no wonder that we can become so confused and disjointed within ourselves.

The Garden of Eden framework – the idea that we are all innately sinners – uses guilt as a weapon through the vehicle of heavy and authoritarian language.

*'You ought to have done your homework.'*
*'You should be kinder to John.'*
*'You must do your hair.'*

These are all forms of authoritarian language that come from our parents, teachers, preachers, and the other authority figures we meet through our lives (and which they, in turn, inherited from their own upbringing). Essentially, this kind of language governs with guilt and duty.

Instead of saying, 'I must go and see Sarah because she's waiting for me', I tried changing the language slightly: 'I am going to do my best to see Sarah.' That tiny change of language shifted my body–mind relationship enormously. 'I've got to... I should have... I must...' – bit by bit, I replaced all of these pressurising words with: 'I will do my best to...'

Doesn't sound like much?

It's changed my life.

In removing the guilt and anxiety of not being good enough, I realised that I didn't have to panic and try to save everyone; I could
be myself and do the best that I could by just being me. It has since
taken me years and years of practice to unwind the language of
centuries past in both my ancestral being and the collective Christian guilt I inherited.

I still achieved a huge amount, but I removed the stress from my
mind. This, in turn, liberated my creativity to do so much more
and allowed me to remain true to myself.

Simply 'being' in the moment, the way I perceive it, means that
*you are you.* You are complete. You have no need to alter or shift
anything or anyone. Crucially this means you must take away the
over-promoted notion of 'I must be my best self' because everyone
will perceive your 'best' differently, and then you run yourself rag-
ged trying to please everyone, which is impossible.

Learning to just be is a journey in itself. It can be a long and con-
fusing path for each of us to be happy 'just being' while constant-
ly challenged by obligations, duties, and stresses. Like most things
in life, I've found that the simpler the notion, the more likely it is
to take years to develop a true understanding and daily practice.
Yet, as exasperating as the 'learning through living' process may
be, I can appreciate the necessity for it.

I'm not suggesting that you shouldn't try to do good, to improve
yourself, to learn more, or to help people. My aim here is to point
out that these are infinitely separate arrows within the quiver of
humanity – and they all stem from the first element of just being.

Get out of your own way, and let the being be.

# Love and Respect Nature

*"All plants are our brothers and sisters.*
*They talk to us and, if we listen, we can hear them"*
— **ARAPAHO PROVERB.**

Everything is connected within Nature, which is why we need to be kind to all of it.

Nature has always had a calming yet inspirational effect on me. Its wondrous seasons drew me to gardens, where I could watch the flora and fauna adapt, conquer, thrive, and just *be*.

Gardens are my happy place; they always have been. From climbing trees to watching a flower grow and guessing what colour petals will emerge, I have always felt such a pure joy from being in a garden.

And yet I never decided that I was a 'gardener' as such, I simply loved – and still love – seeing things grow. Through watching nature, I learnt that gardening itself is love. It's nurturing.

This love of gardening began in the early 1970s in Lebanon, before the civil war. One day, I rescued fifteen discarded palm trees from the side of the road and planted them in my garden. Seeing these big trees that had been around for so many years simply cast aside by people with their bulldozers to create a new highway made me ache inside. I felt I had to save them.

With care and attention, I nurtured them, and they became strong and beautiful again. I even tied evil-eye beads on ribbons around them for protection. I, too, learnt from the trees: I learnt patience, how to adapt, and how to care. Trees are wise, their roots run deep and are interconnected. If one is suffering, the others send vital nutrients to its aid.

When we were bombed out of our house my heart broke, but it broke again when I saw those same trees later used as target practice. I felt the trees' pain because I loved them. They were like my children.

My love for plants and trees endured nonetheless. Today, each plant in my garden represents the best and freest aspects of love. They are the living epitome of 'in the being the doing gets done'.

Sometimes the flowers bloom, other times they don't, and sometimes they die. I cannot think of a stronger metaphor for life and love.

If you give the plants everything they need, they can flourish and be themselves.

Each flower blooms proudly in its own right, unconcerned about what is next to it. Their roots do not compete for nutrients but rather cooperate fiercely to exchange them, until they grow tall and shine, their colours vivid for all to appreciate. They remind me to not compare myself to others and simply bloom in my own right.

# The Power of Purpose

Joseph Campbell, a brilliant thinker and author who worked at the intersection of mythology, spirituality, and psychology, remarked that it is *us* who bring meaning to life; that *we* are the answer to the vast question of our purpose.

Purpose goes beyond what society expects of you; it defines you. Purpose makes an impact.

We get so caught up in plans and being busy yet, as Thoreau said: 'It is not enough to be busy; so are the ants. The question is: what are you busy about?'

You are never too old to discover, create, and become your purpose in life on this Earth. And please know that you can find or redirect your purpose at any given moment.

I was sixty when I found mine. Reaching it often takes great periods of time, despair, and frustration; it certainly did for me.

People have often said to me, 'Alexandra, you are just so certain with your work.' And I nod, because at this point in time I am.

Purpose is something that has both consumed and electrified me. It's also something that has grown and changed over time, and it requires reflection. I've found that people are often uncomfortable with the idea of uncertainty during the process of finding their purpose – but they are charmed by the end result.

I despise feeling stagnant when I know there is much to do. Perhaps you feel the same. And yet I know that I can't force the answers to come to me. I must simply just be.

No one understood this about me better than my good friend and co-conspirator Chuck Spezzano, a leading psychotherapist. While we were working together in the Middle East, I'd been asking him what he believed my life's purpose to be. I was about to turn sixty, and I felt an overwhelming pressure to work it out. But despite my insistence, I got no answer. Just before my birthday, in June 1997, I attended Chuck's two-week seminar on the Psychology of Vision theory on Vancouver Island, Canada. Over these two weeks, Chuck became so frustrated with my continuing to ask if he knew what my purpose was that he quite dramatically banished me – or so it felt – to a period of pure solitude for three days after the seminar in order to find it.

Right, I thought, let's do this. I recall going back to Chuck on several occasions, explaining to him my newly found purpose. 'No,' he would answer, 'that is not your purpose.'

With my sixtieth birthday less than twenty-four hours away, I remember feeling utter despair. I would never find my purpose; it was too convoluted, too big a task. On the verge of giving up, I had a sudden vision of an angel. The angel said: 'I will give you five clues: surrender, willingness, trust, courage, and ask for miracles.' I awoke on my birthday with a clear mind. I was ready to let go and allow my purpose to naturally find me.

In this state of mind, I asked God for guidance by asking a question that had been on my mind: 'Do the living hold the dead, or do the dead hold the living?' Immediately I had a 'beyond the brain' experience confirming an inner understanding. It was overwhelming. Every cell of my body was charged with energy, purpose, and wonder. It was in that moment that I finally knew what my purpose was:

I had to do my best to help break the cycles of violence seen in countries such as my beloved Lebanon. I knew that by healing the generational wounds that people through history had inflicted, I could instil hope for a more forgiving and peaceful future. As immense as it seemed, I felt in every part of my being that I could make it possible.

As you seek your own purpose, remember that you can't force the answers to come to you; you must simply be: surrender, trust, have courage, ask for miracles. Don't be satisfied until every fibre of your being resonates with the conclusion.

# The Power of Joy

Joy is a wonderful, life-affirming feeling. It is a drop of love to your mind.

Discover what brings you joy.

Whether it's a cup of your favourite tea, a song sung to you, a text from a family member, a view of a garden, the promise of travel, laughter, a hug from a friend, or a really good book.

Joy comes in moments, so when you know what brings you joy you can make sure you find it in moments every single day.

Plan for it if you need to, but be aware that the potential for joy is all around you – even on the darkest of days and from the most unexpected sources.

So always be open to receiving joy.

# Anger

It's OK to feel angry, but try to be conscious of what is making you angry and why.

Anger is a response to another hurt. Maybe you've been left out, ignored, or betrayed.

Feel the feeling and ask: what is it trying to tell me?

Then ask yourself: is it worth listening to? Do you want to keep listening to it repeat itself, or do you want to hear it and let it go?

When you do eventually act, try to act out of love with the goal of finding peace in your own mind. If not love for the thing or person who hurt you, then at least love for yourself.

By embracing the part of yourself that's been ignored or hurt, you can help dissolve the anger.

# Hate

Hate doesn't enter my story much. Honestly, it's a complete waste of time. It sends you charging in the wrong direction.

When you want to achieve good things in this life, you'll find that hate doesn't help you do that.

If someone has done something wrong, perhaps even barbaric, to you or your family, it may be natural to feel hate toward them – as though somehow, such hate might mitigate our pain or lead one day to justice.

But having hate in your heart doesn't lead to anything good. Even if you're sitting alone, it will poison your own peace. Focus instead on a positive way out of the situation you're in by transcending the dynamic in which you find yourself.

We all have the capacity to think about this predicament from another level.

We all live on the wrong side of somebody's fence. Our goal is to remember that these fences are very often arbitrary, put there in the past by someone remote from us in our lives today – perhaps with good intentions, but without awareness of the effects these fences would have.

I was raised hating the Germans and the Japanese because we were at war with them, and they with us. That hate had more to do with my being born into a particular group than it did with my actual understanding of the wider reasons for war and the hate that ensued.

I was first a target of 'hateful' acts in my childhood when I was bombed in the Blitz and spent many nights in flooded bomb shelters. Later in my life I lived through another war – this time in Lebanon after I married a Lebanese Christian – with people I didn't know or understand: the Palestinians, the Syrians, the Israelis, and the Americans.

It is better to understand the roots of violence and hatred. Whether it is our own or that of others, we are all susceptible to entering a collective (essentially natural) habit of hating the 'other'. But doing so traps us and condemns us to a cycle of revenge.

In the end, I chose not to participate in the endless cycles of war. I gave it neither my feelings nor my reactions. Instead, I looked for ways to shift my own energy and, through connection with others, theirs too.

Two former militia fighters from Lebanon – one Christian (Assaad), the other Sunni Muslim (Muhieddine) – had been raised from childhood with distrust and hatred of the other. They both entered the civil war as militiamen in their twenties, and killing became a livelihood justified through these inherited narratives. As part of my work in the Healing the Wounds of History programme, I was seeking people who'd participated in the war. I eventually brought Assaad and Muhieddine together – men who'd literally fired rockets at one another thirty-three years prior – and we travelled across America talking to different communities to explain their journeys through the tragedy of war: inherited hatred, mindless violence, and eventually (through much deeper awareness) the capacity to grow and forgive.

Hate is not good food. You have many other choices for moving through pain. Choose instead to nourish yourself with higher awareness, understanding, and love.

Your descendants will bless you.

# Envy and Jealousy

You'll always see people around you who have more than you in some way. Who are more successful, richer, fitter, or healthier – the list goes on. That's life. I accept this.

First, just recognising that fact takes the pressure off.

Second, remember that you are unique: you've landed on Earth in a unique place. You've inherited a kaleidoscope of talents, limitations, and complexities that are invisible to others. Embrace them all and be proud to make the most of what you have.

Focus on your own unique talents and enjoy *being you*; enjoy who you are and what you have. Do your best within your means.

If you want something, work hard for it. Then be pleased with your progress. And build on top of it. Achievements are relative and context dependent. They cannot be compared.

Let the achievements of others inspire you, then focus on you. Envy or jealousy are a waste – not just of time, but of emotional energy.

# Guilt

If one of my grandchildren came to me and said that they felt guilty, I'd give them a hug immediately.

It's OK to feel guilty. In fact, it is good: it shows empathy. I wouldn't want them to feel overly worried, so I'd treat them with compassion – not anger for whatever it is they felt guilty about – and give them a safe space to unload.

Making mistakes is part of the human journey.

Be sorry for doing wrong by someone and then move on, without doing it again.

This helps us to move beyond thinking of ourselves as a victim, a persecutor, or a saviour.

These presumed identities are fuelled by our own fears about ourselves.

As we become more accepting, forgiving, and compassionate with ourselves, we can let go of and dissolve these negative energies and cease to project them onto others.

A person should never be reduced to their trauma or guilt – and that includes you.

# Letting Go

Letting go of any negative thoughts enables us to create positive cycles for our lives and for those around us. This is especially the case for our children, who might otherwise be influenced by our negativity.

There are many ways to let go: some favour talking through it, some favour a long walk by the sea, while others might turn to meditation or body work, such as yoga.

Discover what helps you to let things go and be excited to do it.

It's important to note that letting go is not the same as forgetting. You don't need to forget something to let it go.

Whatever it is that you need to let go of, remember what you learnt from it, and then release the hurt.

# When You Don't Feel Warmth From Your Parents

If you've not felt warmth from your parents, my heart goes out to you.

It's an incredibly sad feeling. But it's often not their fault... or yours.

Warmth comes from warmth, so if their own parents haven't shown them how to be loving then they will struggle to share love with you. They may just not know *how*.

While it might feel unfair to show them warmth first, just start doing it.

If they completely reject it, it's not personal.

And, as hard as that might be to understand, it's to do with them and not you.

Find a partner or friend to give you the warmth, understanding, and love you need.

Keep giving your parents hugs – after a while, you might find that they won't let go.

# Transforming Pity or Guilt

Try not to look at those in poverty or misery with pity or guilt. Pity and guilt are not transformative forces. They are diminishing to you and those you're judging.

Look instead with love and acceptance.

This will allow you to proceed with a pure heart and to share your joy and lightness with others.

# Kindness to Strangers

My grandparents escaped Russia during the revolution and eventually settled in southern France. During World War Two, they were always on the run from the occupying German troops. Without the aid and kindness of local French villagers at every juncture, they would not have survived.

From early warnings of incoming Gestapo to help moving around, provision of secret shelters, food, and other supplies: even during such a high-stakes period of the war, these acts of kindness and self-lessness from strangers – who had *everything* to lose – kept my grandparents alive. This human story has stayed with me for my whole life.

From an early age, I've noticed the benefits of people's instinct to pull together – to provide help and kindness to other people, to animals, indeed all living things. My father used his gifts and talents to serve his country as a naval officer. My mother was always hunting for ways to be, in her words, 'useful', even driving ambulances in London during the Blitz.

Everyone on this Earth, including you, has a unique set of skills or qualities that can help ease suffering and bring hope to those needing it – in moments of war, pain, difficulty, or otherwise, and to strangers as well as to friends.

Your acts of kindness towards others light up the world and set an example for the rest of us to do the same.

# Fear and Trust

*"Trust in Allah, but tie your camel"*
**- ARABIC PROVERB**

When I was a little girl, I would leap into my bed to evade the imagined ghosts that hid in the darkness underneath it. I later realised that what I feared was the unknown.

Fear is an instinct to protect ourselves from danger. Fear can lead to paralysis or to courage.

To have courage is to acknowledge your fear so you can step through it – to have the capacity to move beyond it. If you're lucky, life will allow you to meet your fears without them overwhelming you.

Fear is used by our leaders – by parents, teachers, newspapers, and politicians; anyone who, in a sense, takes charge of the narrative – as one of their prime powers of control and, often, as tools of manipulation.

Every society has its ghosts.

*Beware of those people.*
*Don't trust that country.*

Many families (including my own) are raised with fear as a background to their lives.

*Don't try this, don't try that.*
*Don't go to the Jones' house, they have a dangerous dog.*
*Avoid Jimmy. He's from the wrong family.*
*Don't climb that fence, it might break.*

The positive intention of that fear is to keep us safe. However, if fear is all we have, we become paralysed as individuals, as groups, and as a society. We just don't move forward.

The alternative is not to be irresponsible with real danger, but to take due care mentally and physically so that you can develop the appropriate confidence to face the danger or the risks.

Trust tends to come from our upbringing. If we are lucky enough to have people around us in our early years to encourage us to take the next leap (whatever that might be) with a sense of safety, this breeds confidence.

You can trust that you have the capacity to jump the fence. And then you must jump the fence. This is part of risk-taking.

If you don't face danger, however big or small, you won't develop any strengths. This applies not just to the physical sphere, but to the cerebral world and to relationships. It is only through trying and trusting that the world will teach you something that you can ever hope to make real progress.

When I was eighteen years old, I took a boat from London to Montreal and found myself a copywriting job, trusting that I would be able to find my way and learn through doing. I had, in a sense, overcome the fear of being marooned in London in a mundane job.

When I came back, I built on that confidence and trust in myself to keep growing. Eventually, in 1957, I became the first female copywriter in one of the largest advertising agencies at the time.

Trust is about creating confidence in our ability to navigate the real dangers without missing out on the opportunity and serendipity that await us in life. Through this confidence, we are encouraged to try new adventures, we take due care, and we trust ourselves to navigate whatever will come to pass.

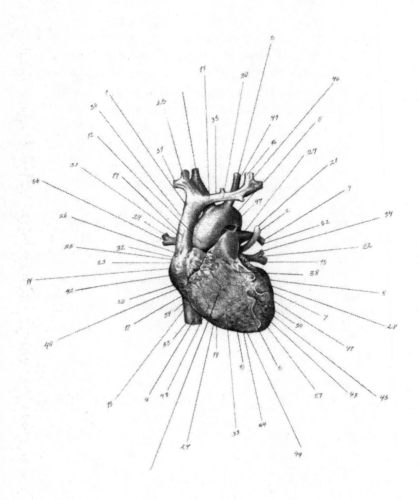

# Love in All Its Forms

L ove is the absolute essence of being alive. I'm smiling even as I write this because I know with my whole being that this statement is true.

You can't grab at love. It's an expression of a feeling.

You will feel love many times, I hope, and in many different ways.

Let yourself feel love; it's warm honey. If it's felt by someone else towards you, they will express it to you in their own way. But it must come naturally. It can't be forced.

Every person's perception of love is different. It might be based on what we've experienced as a child or what we wished we'd experienced. Romantic stories and fairy tales can either confirm or distort our vision of love, and very often popular culture makes us believe that finding 'the one' is the only version of love.

Of course, it's not.

There are so many varieties of love in life; if you are open to them, you can never be without love. Every part of your life can encompass love if you simply make the choice to live your life in that way.

In dark times, love has pulled me through – love for my family, love for my community, love for my friends, colleagues, animals, beliefs, you name it. I've loved and continue to love.

It is my wish for you that you let yourself love in as many ways as possible.

Love animals, people, mountains, trees, the tiniest of flowers, the sound of laughter, and the feeling when inspiration hits. Be so full of love that when something bad happens, as it so often does in life, you react with love, not hate or vengeance.

And when you can love, love becomes a magnet. Love begets love.

Like the universe, love is alive, and sharing it heightens the energy around you to attract more. Each natural warm act may encourage another's warm response or warm up a cold heart.

That's not to say that love can't be tested. Love in every form can be manipulated, destroyed, tested, rebuilt, and questioned. Quite often it can be a challenge to steady one's mind against the effects of unloving actions that are dressed up as love.

Just remember: if love feels unkind, it's not love. Love, even tough love, is inherently kind.

Love gives birth to other emotions – forgiveness, peace, joy, pain, excitement, heartbreak, hope, and safety. All these can stem from feelings of great love. I've learnt not to force them, nor to run from them, but to feel them to my bones and trust that at some point they will make sense.

The highs of love can also lead to crashing falls and periods of lows. Heartbreak holds you back from accepting the blessings that are truly meant for you. I hope that you work through any love-related scars within you so that you can love, learn, live, and love again.

We often don't receive love because we don't love or believe in ourselves. If you find love is locked out of your heart, make forgiveness the key and allow compassion to thrive. To love wholeheartedly, you need to be able to receive it wholeheartedly.

Start with loving yourself and then do your best to notice the myriad ways in which others can share their love with *you*.

Love doesn't have to be loud. I've been surrounded by people who have been inherently kind and shown their love through quiet acts of kindness.

Love instils patience, which helps you to look for the positive intention behind someone's acts.

And love can be a catalyst for change.

Love is the answer even if it doesn't carry all the answers.

Acting with love will guide you to what is meant to be yours.

# Releasing the Unquiet Dead

In 1978 I went to a conference for Subud – an international, interfaith spiritual movement – in Spokane, Washington, where I was asked during a workshop, 'Do you want to ask any questions of God?' (Because that is the way we do it.)

I said, 'Yes, I've got a question for God. Is there a contract between the living and the dead? Do the dead hold the living, and the living hold the dead?'

It was casual and irreverent. It was a cheeky question. But the response within me to that question was so gigantic, so enormous, so life-changing for me. It was as if every single cell in my body shifted. Every vein, every bone, every particle inside of me felt like it was put through 55 million volts.

I realised I was onto something: that we keep repeating what our ancestors or our collective group has always done – hate these people, distrust those, admire others again. The unfinished business of our ancestors is placed on us unconsciously.

It is my belief that, for the most part, these are often the ancestors who are still caught in war, who are still fighting at some level even in their afterlife. They are still involved, they are still caught in the anger at being killed in battle, being killed as an innocent, or being displaced. They did not have a chance to understand and forgive before they died, so they are stuck in that rage.

And the echoes of this rage, despair, or misunderstandings affect us as their descendants.

If someone has passed unpeacefully, their soul might stay around until it is heard. I call these 'beings' the unquiet dead. You release the unquiet dead by allowing the energy of that person to talk. It is like doing therapy with the dead.

I was intrigued, so I began reading a lot of books by the psychiatrist Kenneth McCall about healing family trees and working with prisoners of war in Japan. He had been a prisoner of war himself, and during his imprisonment he noticed a lot of things about those who survived and those who didn't and, in particular, the energy that surrounded death. I went to many of his workshops and they were fascinating.

Later, a group of his sailed in a boat to the Bermuda Triangle, which is on an old slave shipping route. They heard the wailing of enslaved people who had been cast overboard because they were ill, pregnant, or too young or old to be sold. The group performed spiritual rituals and released them.

I felt naturally drawn to this, so I joined a group called the Psychic Task Force, led by Roger Woolger, a marvellous Jungian therapist and good friend of mine, alas no longer with us. Together, we'd go to battlefields and release the unquiet dead.

On one trip we went to Ireland, where we found ourselves swarmed by angry souls. When asked to speak, the souls conveyed that they had been deceived and killed by the British. They had experienced horrific betrayal and humiliation, emotions so common in war and violent occupation. Our group did an exercise to release these souls, and we felt them all ascend together.

Many years later I had my own experiences with the unquiet dead.

One day I felt a tapping on my shoulder and had a strange feeling that it was my uncle, Richard, who had died aged sixteen in the battle of Jutland, long before I was born. I felt he must be in trouble somewhere; I prayed for him with the intention of acknowledging his trauma and releasing him from it. Moments later, I felt him liberated.

Soon after this experience, I saw a photo in *The Independent* of five young men in uniform, survivors of the battle of Jutland. Aged sixteen in the photo, they were now 100. I wished I could get in contact with one of them. Auspiciously, the next day I bumped into a relative of a survivor by chance at a lunch. I was invited to meet his great uncle, who recalled his time during the battle seeing bodies in the water and cheering, thinking they were Germans.

I believe this is why my uncle had an unquiet death. He was wondering why he was not being saved by his countrymen; he felt betrayed and unseen in his final moments. That pain of feeling unnoticed, unseen, and unsaved can echo through generations of a family, until it is acknowledged and healed.

Years later I had another experience, this time with my late grandmother. In her life she had been very cold and never showed affection, even to my father. I do believe she loved me, despite her coldness. It suddenly struck me that she was still completely locked in by heartbreak from the loss of her son, my uncle. This heartbreak had shut out her husband and her two remaining sons (my father and his brother). I felt I wanted to reunite them all. And in that moment, I saw her cold exterior crumble around her, and I felt the love that had been locked in for so long come flowing out like hot sticky honey. It was a beautiful, visceral experience.

If we can resolve the anger and despair of our ancestors that is cemented in us, we can be free to focus on being ourselves and let our love and human potential flow freely – for ourselves and future generations.

Alexandra Asseily

# Healing the Wounds
# of History

Jonas Salk, the brilliant virologist and father of the Polio
vaccine, once remarked that being responsible ancestors is
perhaps our most important legacy as human beings.

How do we become good ancestors and refrain from passing on
trauma or negative beliefs to future generations?

How do we stop being the prisoners and the puppets of the
stinging memories of strife that we can still feel today?

How do we clean up what I call our 'ancestral arteries' so that
our children can act freely in the present, untethered from the
blocks that echo from the past and that clog up our present
and future?

The goal is to let history inform us, not control us.

Who we are today can be shaped by several past generations.
No one is born with hate within them, but family and societal
influences and beliefs are instilled from a young age. If we are
imbued with hate, fear, and violence, the cycle will inevitably
begin all over again.

Unconscious inherited narratives can continue to pass on

trans-generationally through unresolved trauma. Our narratives and emotions are often echoed from the past. We are therefore often being narrated, rather than narrating ourselves. Most of these painful stories are what we indeed believe to be true, and we base our lives upon these illusions – until we can see them for what they are and release them, along with the grievances of our ancestors and our society's collective memory.

We can change 'history' not only for ourselves as individuals but for our families, groups, tribes, or nations. Through love and forgiveness, we can become the narrator. We can become good ancestors.

In 2011, I made the decision to take all that I'd learnt from my understanding of psychotherapy and life experiences – in and beyond war – as well as our findings at the Centre for Lebanese Studies and my own belief in forgiveness, to create a three-day international conference on generational trauma. It was held at the University of Balamand near Byblos, Lebanon. My aim was to raise consciousness and inspire people on their own journeys to love and forgiveness in Lebanon. This had never been done before. Yet I believed deeply that it would work, that it needed to work. We had to find a way to break these communitarian cycles of violence with tools we had been using at the individual level. During the conference, we created workshops for this purpose. I called them Healing the Wounds of History (HWH). Politicians, students, teachers, and NGO leaders all came. For the next eight years, we continued to hold HWH workshops yearly in Lebanon for people around the world.

In the workshops, we heard testimonies from former guerrilla and militia fighters and their survivors, from Lebanon and beyond. Then, working with the participants from these communities, we listened to their individual stories of pain, confusion, loss, and grief – the stings of trauma. We spoke about the unspeakable, we listened, and we all agreed that we never wanted to see the acts of the preceding thirty years ever again.

We must learn to release the stings of trauma we hold in our memories. In doing so, we can encourage each other and wider groups to create a political space for real, in-depth reconciliation.

Healing the trauma within a single person begins to heal the trauma within all the people that person subsequently encounters. As each of us follows the path to forgiveness and healing, we can block the propagation of hate.

## How to heal the wounds of your own history:

The steps from the HWH workshops encourage a general spiritual awakening and awareness of our divine inner voice. They can be followed by anyone who wishes to develop a greater awareness of the need for harmony and the capacity to manifest it in our lives.

### Step 1: *Taking responsibility*
Begin by taking responsibility for your own part in any conflict/ imbalance/tension/grievance/problem with courage, honesty, and humility – even if you do not feel personally involved in or responsible for the conflict.

### Step 2: *Asking and reflecting*
Sit or stand quietly for 4–6 minutes. Relax and allow thoughts to come and go in order to clear your mind of the day's events.

Then ask yourself the following questions (pick either harmony or ancestral beliefs).

### *On harmony*

**1.** What is peace and harmony for me?

**2.** In what way am I preventing peace and harmony in and around me?

**3.** What is the special gift (spiritual or physical) am I not yet fully using to bring healing in and around me?

**4.** In what way am I preventing harmony within my body?

**5.** What is the gift am I not yet using to bring harmony to my body?

Repeat questions 4 and 5, replacing the word 'body' with other relevant words, such as: self, family, work, group, nation, and world. Then, finally, ask yourself:

**6.** In what way am I preventing harmony with [name of the person/s with whom I have the greatest conflict]?

### On ancestral beliefs

**1.** What do I model or inherit from my father's family line, which is no longer appropriate?

**2.** What do I model or inherit from my father, which is no longer appropriate?

**3.** What do I model or inherit from my mother's family line, which is no longer appropriate?

**4.** What do I model or inherit from my mother, which is no longer appropriate?

*Ask for grace and a sense of an inner awareness of forgiveness for ourselves, our parents, and our ancestors.*

**1.** What is the gift from my father's family line, which I am not yet fully using in my life at this time?

**2.** What is the gift from my father, which I am not yet fully using in my life at this time?

**3.** What is the gift from my mother's family line, which I am not yet fully using in my life at this time?

**4.** What is the gift from my mother, which I am not yet fully using in my life at this time?

Ask each question internally and wait patiently. The reply may come in a variety of ways: a picture, a series of images, words in your mind, words written on an internal screen, a feeling, thoughts, or a combination of all or some of these responses.

Reflect for a few moments on what has been received and to distil your inner understanding.

### Step 3: *Forgiving*
By understanding and allowing for forgiveness of oneself and others – including our ancestors and our collective past – we can let go of guilt, shame, and fear. We then no longer need to uphold, consciously or unconsciously, the same grievances from one generation to another. As we forgive others, we forgive ourselves and vice versa.

Many of us resist forgiveness because of the feeling that we may be letting a significant other or others off the hook and helping them to avoid justice, and betraying our obligations to our ancestors or our collective past. Also, many of us resist forgiving because we have been so badly hurt, and fear forgetting our pain and suffering. This resistance blocks us from fully expressing our own gifts and handing them on to our children.

### Step 4: *Understanding our authentic selves and releasing*
Throughout the process of forgiveness, we must listen to our inner wisdom. This will tell us what changes we can make in order to speak with our own 'inner cohesive authority', sometimes called our 'higher mind' (as opposed to our fractured, reactive, self). Then, we can release within ourselves all obstacles that prevent us from promoting harmony or being able to speak with our own voice, within ourselves and with each other.

*Note: asking for release can be done at any time in the process.*

**Step 5: *Sharing***
Finally, by sharing this healing process with others, we can transform not just ourselves but our families and our communities.

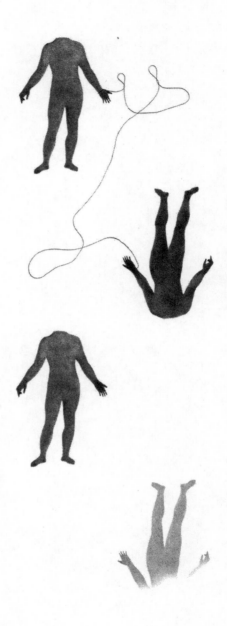

# The Power of Forgiveness

F orgiving is a conscious act.

The Beirut I know and love was shredded by its civil war from 1975 to 1990. In Lebanon, religion also means identity, tribe, and community. There are officially sixteen different religious communities in Lebanon, all of which have been in conflict with each other at various times. The immensity of suffering on all sides is difficult to comprehend. For many, the idea of forgiveness was – and still is – unthinkable.

But holding onto anger and resentment harms both mind and body. Indeed, the physical effects of stress and trauma on our health are significant.

Forgiveness allows for healing past and present wounds. It's about releasing those negative emotions, freeing up space and energy, and embracing peace.

It opens up opportunities for life, love, and kindness.

It was in this spirit that, one day in August 1998, I had a vision for a garden at the centre of Beirut. A garden open to all, a place of inclusion, not clouded by social, political, religious, or financial motives. It would be the Garden of Forgiveness.

I wanted it to inspire the concept of forgiveness in a country that had suffered through centuries of internal conflict. And through embracing forgiveness, our communities could eventually heal and co-exist peacefully.

After many years working alongside local religious and political authorities in Lebanon, a magical space was set aside in the centre of Beirut. The Garden of Forgiveness would be wedged between three mosques, three cathedrals, and it would sit above ancient Roman and Byzantine ruins. Nestled within the site is a fourth-century shrine to the Virgin Mary (revered and visited by women of all faiths in Lebanon). I then began working with the Beirut authorities and landscape designers to create a garden that would respect the layers of history underfoot and manifest a powerful spirit of reflection, peace, and forgiveness. Though the garden itself remains incomplete, the project has already touched the hearts and lives of many who have been involved. After all, we can all be freed by forgiveness.

*** 

Emotional responses to hurt are personal.

In my work, I've discussed humanity's capacity for cruelty and the ease with which we resort to violence. Violent reactions to provocations – from individuals to superpowers – often stem from personal or collective fear. Terrorism and authoritarian rule often go hand in hand, with violence begetting more violence. And historical grievances, like the aftermath of wars and humiliations, often foster vengefulness. The subsequent anger, blame, and desire for revenge can lead to a repetition of conflict.

But our higher selves know that revenge only leads to further darkness, as Gandhi warns with his principle 'an eye for an eye makes the whole world go blind'. Likewise, Jesus' teaching to

turn the other cheek may seem outlandish to many, but it addresses the root of authoritarianism and violence.
Reconciliation shows us that forgiveness can overcome shame and heal societies.

It can mark the end of mourning, recognising pain and loss. Forgiveness, not vengeance, is the path to true peace.

True forgiveness is not about removing culpability. It is about preventing the sins of others from taking charge of us and steering our future lives. This doesn't imply that we don't take steps to protect ourselves from the same events being repeated. Forgiveness is about ensuring you, your children, and your community don't become perpetual victims of the past by remaining trapped in anger, hate, and shame.

In a sense, it is about restoring innocence.

Every religion has its own take on who has the right to forgive and be forgiven. But we cannot always depend on religion for guidance: forgiveness and healing are fundamental human processes that transcend doctrine.

It is our own ability to react without blame or shame that will define who we are and that will help us seek peace instead of revenge.

Consider Ho'oponopono, an ancient Hawaiian practice of reconciliation and forgiveness, which emphasises personal responsibility for healing. I think of forgiveness as a self-healing process, which results in benefits for oneself and for all.

Forgiveness therefore is ultimately an act of self-preservation. It is a gift, not to be bestowed on others by us (or by others on us) but to be received as a grace by surrendering our pain. It must be offered to ourselves and others – and even to events beyond our control – with a willing and open heart. Our freedom comes when we realise that, in order to thrive, survive, and break out of our prisons of resentments and hate, we have no other choice but to forgive and live our true purpose – fully alive and unshackled by trauma and resentment.

It is in this way that we become good ancestors.

# ONLINE RESOURCES AND FURTHER READING

• *alexandraasseily.org*

• Ara Pacis Initiatives for Peace: *arapacis.org*

• Asseily, Alexandra. 2007. *Breaking the Cycles of Violence in Lebanon – and Beyond*. Brighton: Guerrand-Hermès Foundation for Peace Publishing.

• Asseily, Alexandra. 2012. *The Power of Language: How Small Shifts in Language Create Big Shifts in Relationships and Behaviour*. In Rethinking Education for Social Cohesion: International Case Studies, edited by Maha Shuayb. London: Palgrave Macmillan.

• Bsous Silk Museum: *thesilkmuseum.com*

• Centre for Lebanese Studies: *lebanesestudies.com*

• Guerrand-Hermès Foundation for Peace: *ghfp.org*

• Center for the Study of World Religions, Harvard Divinity School: *cswr.hds.harvard.edu*

• Harvard Divinity School: *hds.harvard.edu*

• Healing the Wounds of History: *healingwoundsofhistory.com*